A, B, See the Beatles!

A, B, See the Beatles!

A Children's ABC Book

Written by

Jill Davis

Illustrations by

Jeanne Conway

JAD
Decatur, Illinois

To Oliver—
Let it be...
Jill Davis

ISBN-13: 978-0-9861166-0-5
LCCN: 2015906372

Printed in the United States of America

For my grandchildren

Acknowledgments

I would like to thank my beautiful daughter, Amanda Peters, for her advice, ideas and savvy business and technical counsel. Thank you to my lifelong friend, Sue Avery, for being my BFF (Beatle Friend Forever). Thank you to my awesome illustrator, Jeannie, for bringing my vision to life. And thanks to my husband, Dave, who is always my rock and compass.

To my supporters and cheerleaders along the way: Thanks for "a little help from my friends"!

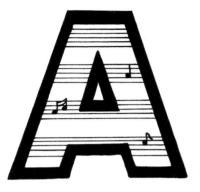 is for Apple,

not the kind you eat.

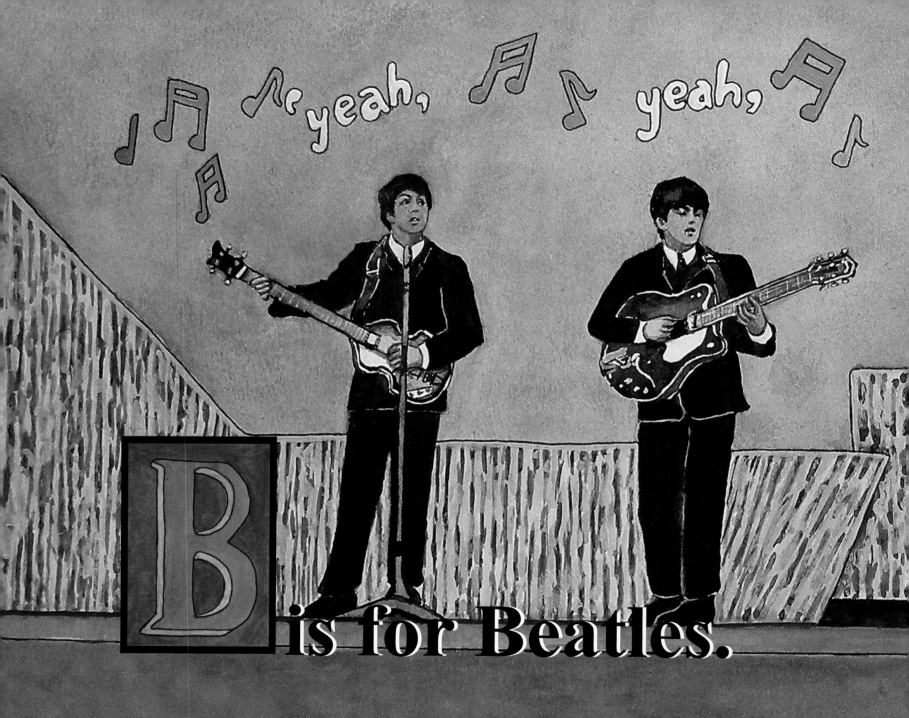

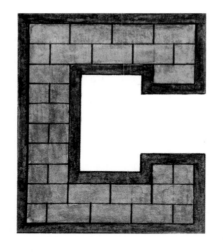 **is for Cavern Club concerts at noon.**

 **is for John and Paul's "Day Tripper" tune.**

 **is for Epstein**

and the eggman, too!

is for
Fab
Four
Forever,
for
you!

is for George and his guitar.

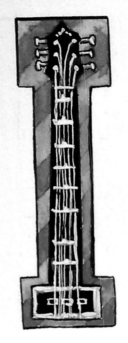 **is for instruments,**

three guitars and a drum.

K is for kooky kaleidoscope eyes.

L is for Liverpool

and its blue suburban skies.

 **is for music,**

a rock 'n' roll plan.

 **is for a real**

"Nowhere Man."

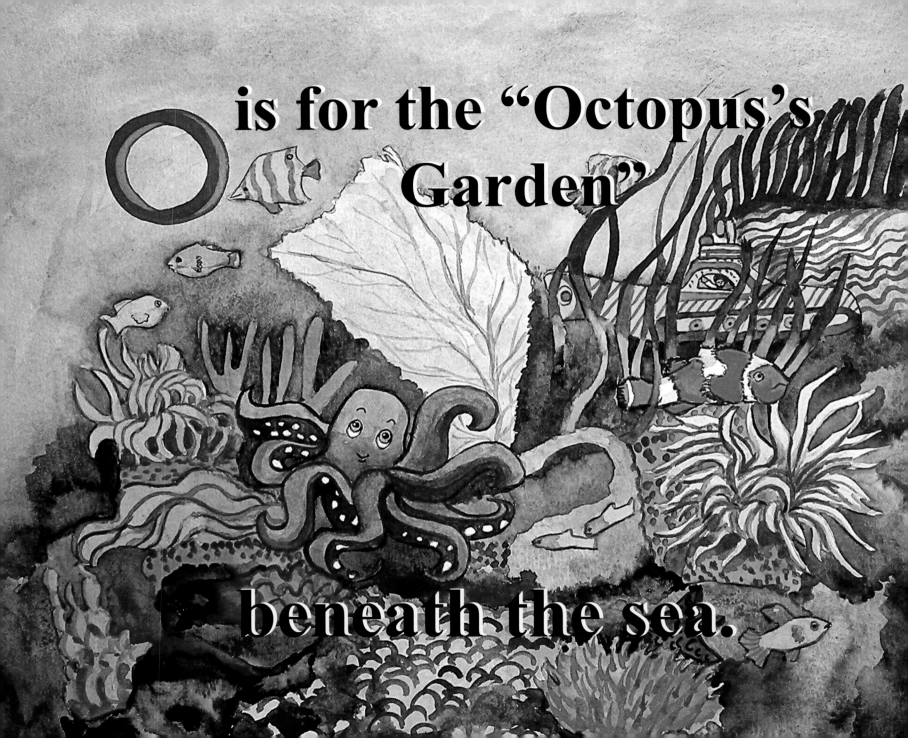

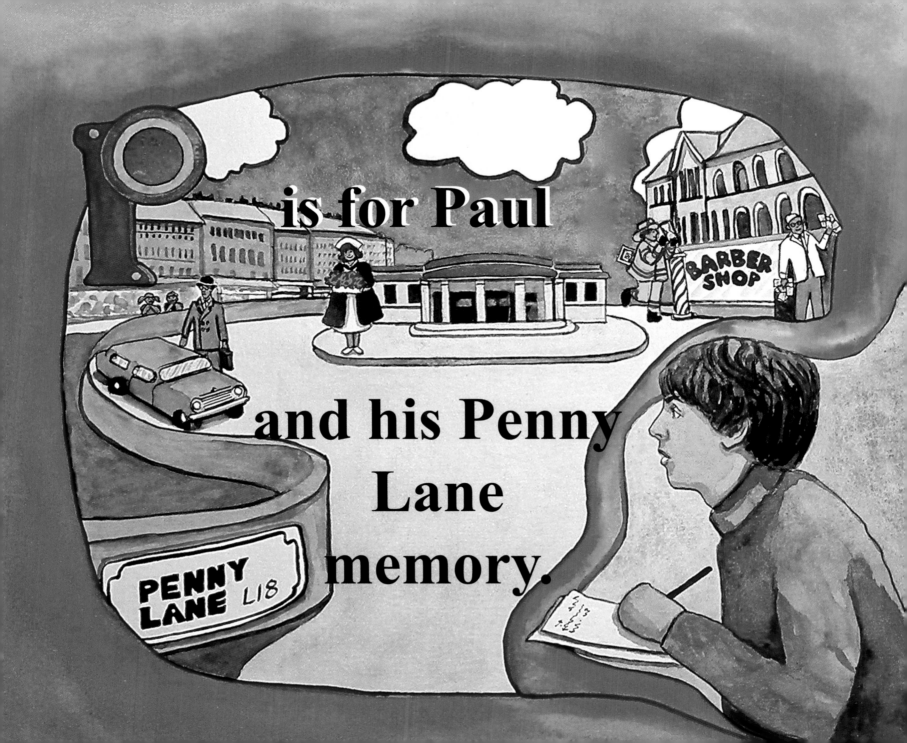

 **is for the Quarrymen**

at the St. Peter's Church fete.

R is for Ringo.

He joined the
Beatles
late!

S is for Stuart in Hamburg long ago.

 **is for the Top Ten Club.**

Club.

What a show!

is for the universe,

that sky-of-diamonds place.

V is for Paul's violin bass.

W is for the "words of wisdom" in

Let it be

"Let It Be."

 is for x-tra love.

"All you need is love,"
you see!

Y is for YOU, for whom

the Beatles still play.

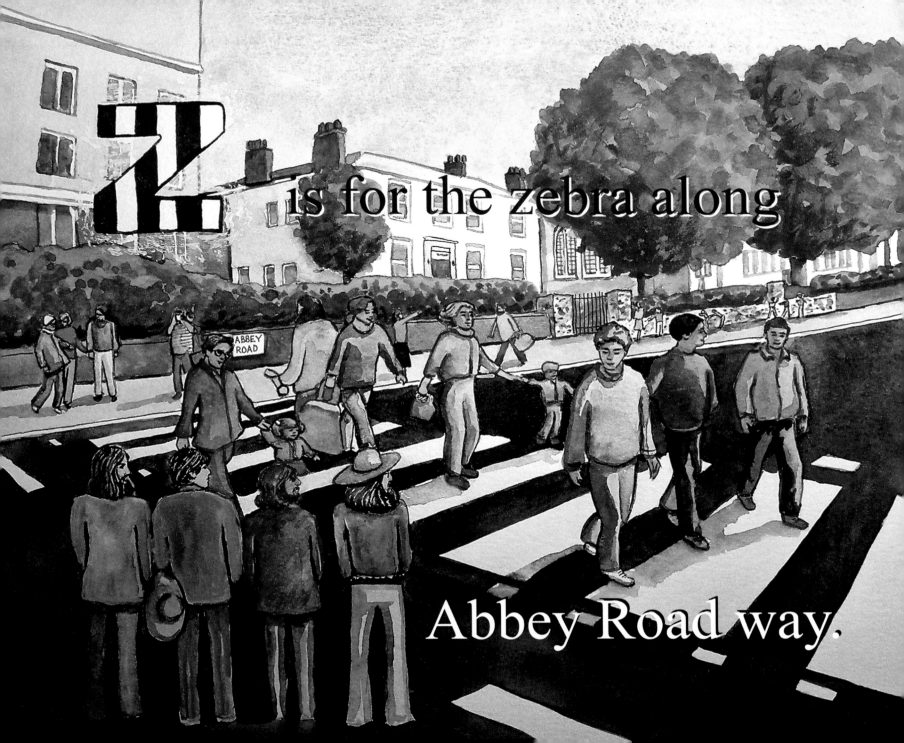

Z is for the zebra along

Abbey Road way.

You've taken this journey through
the Beatles' ABC.
May their music go with you,
wherever you may be!

"And in the end... the love you take... is
equal to the love...you make"
Lennon-McCartney

About the Author

Jill Davis taught elementary school for thirty-three years and has a master's degree in elementary education. She has a love for children's literature, the Beatles and her grandchildren. Upon returning from an overseas Magical History Tour on the Beatles, Davis decided she must share her knowledge and love of the band with her grandchildren and the children of the world. Jill resides in Decatur, Illinois, with her husband, Dave.

About the Illustrator

Jeanne Conway is an artist and also an illustrator, working mostly in watercolors. She is a member of the Society of Children's Book Writers and Illustrators (SCBWI) and most recently illustrated Dina Anastasio's children's book, *The Storm*, published by Pearson Digital Library. In addition to her own art, Conway has been an art teacher for twenty-seven years. She has taught children from the ages of five to eighteen in St. Louis (her hometown) and in London, England. She is currently teaching art at an elementary school in south St. Louis County.